BOUNDED BY INK

COLLECTION II

By

Narell Hunt

ISBN Paperback: 978-1-7352351-3-4
ISBN E-book: 978-1-7352351-5-8

"Bounded by Ink: Collection II" is a poetic free-form novel that also consists of artwork from artists.

Lilac Sky Publishing, LLC

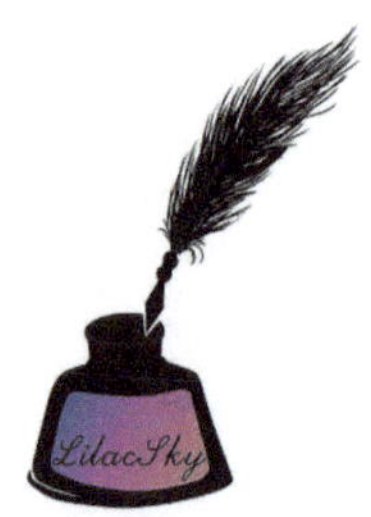

www.lilacskypublishing.com

Also by Author Narell Hunt:

Just My Imagination;
Father, May I: Collection I

To Passion,
If you have not found what moves you, I pray you do, and may it
blossom into your wildest dreams.

"Anything worth building takes time, focus and dedication. Your dreams deserve nothing less."
-Eleanor Brown

Table of Contents

Que Sera Sera

The know-how of not allowing life to get in the way of your dreams is a power not often talked about, and a practice that goes unnoticed. When discussing such a topic, the word balance comes up because as adults, we gain more responsibilities. If our responsibilities aren't handled well, then life can become a bit chaotic. So, we find ways to prioritize our responsibilities, while finding joy in the things we love to do, which is a healthy balance.

Easier said than done.

Being an adult will force you to comply with the norm, school prepares us for it. We learn to pass exams, rather than find joy in what we're learning, ask permission when we need to go to the restroom, meet the expectations of others, and follow a routine - a system, with little to no input as to what we learn. I find it ironic that the same companies who build most of our public schools also build prisons, but that's a topic for another time.

Joy for me comes when I create, and creating takes a certain level of freedom.

What I've been doing is finding that balance. It's no secret that being an entrepreneur is costly and bringing in a consistent paycheck is needed when you're starting out. I'm grateful for that consistency. However, I often beg the question, am I playing it smart or am I scared to let go of the consistency of income and put all my energy into my brand? If I am a woman of God, should I not believe that He will always catch me when I fall and lift me higher when I walk on the path of my dreams? My day job may be a part of this journey, and maybe I shouldn't overthink.

As you can see dear reader, I'm in a battle.

My hope is that all creators, artists, and entrepreneurs who may be facing this same issue, is that we get to a point where doing what we love generates that consistent income, which will allow us to live in abundance, and if you're like most who are still trying to figure it out, remember, Vera Wang didn't design her first dress until she was 40.

What shall be, will always be, working on trusting the process.

"The more you believe and trust God, the more limitless your possibilities become for your family, your career - for your life!"

- Rick Warren

Bounded by Ink

Thoughts keep me up
Moving around like new lovers…
Slow dancing
Can't help how they admire one another.

How tight they hold,
But soon they know
They must release.

Unleashing them unto paper…
Where they can be free,
But still joined together,

Bounded by ink.

With My Life, I Should Write a Book

I've spent valuable time learning lessons,
Time well spent if the lessons are learned I suppose.

Life is full of them,
Lessons that is,
I laugh while reminiscing.

Time to Live

Keeping my mood calm.
I'm one,
I'm whole…
My heart's warm,
You don't want to see it cold…
Breaking this spirit out of
Survival mode.

Takes a special type of journey for this transition.
Jumping into audio so even the blind can see my vision.
Empowerment in my words,
Take the time to listen.

Was the Scapegoat of the family,
So, if I was not liked,
I'm not tripping.

My heart is warm.

You don't want to see it cold,
Breaking this spirit out of
Survival mode
Because it's time to live.

Be Kind to You

*If seven years ago, you would give anything to be in the position
that you're in now, (mentally, physically, financially, or spiritually),
then you are a success! Be proud and talk to yourself kindly.
Lean on your Faith and not of man, for man's imperfect,
and your strength must come from a more powerful source.*

I want to share a message I received from the novel, *Where the Crawdads Sing, by Delia Owens*. The main character is a girl named Kya. Kya has been abandoned by everyone she loved and who she thought loved her. When she meets a man who gives her attention, although yearning for companionship, his forceful nature to be intimate with her rubs Kya the wrong way (literally), and she removes herself from the "gentleman." It's no secret that this character yearns for companionship after many years of living in isolation. However, that did not interfere with the value she had for herself.

After Kya took a stand, the author begs the question, "How much do you trade to defeat lonesomeness?" Companionship is needed, I speak of that in one of my poems titled *Let Nature Sing*, in my first poetry novel, *Father, May I: Collection I*, but your dignity and self-respect should never be traded off.

If you didn't hear it today, I love you and you are not alone.

Anxious Attachments II

There's a young girl I'm trying to remember,
I think about her often.

She used to come out when she didn't get her way.
Like most girls,
She liked to run outside, jump rope, play…
She enjoyed latch hooks.
Still does,
Even 'til this day.

You should see this one she made;
It's a tiger she hangs on the back of her videos for display.

The family had it tough during her years of adolescence.
She learned quickly that life doesn't care about age when it
comes to those hard lessons.

Maybe she's becoming more of a distant memory
Because she's all patched up and goes where the past lives to be free …
Fifth time going through a transformation,
It seems to be every seven years for me.
Will be thirty-five in just a few weeks…

So go be free past me.
Your experiences have prepared us well,
But I now have new memories to share …

New stories to tell.

Who Goes There?

Are they praying or preying?
Must watch their energy,
And the company I keep.
A winner
Had to learn to schedule time for sleep.

I don't sweat,
I glisten.
My face doesn't get red when angered,
That's just how it glows.
When I cry, it's only to let my soul shine,
That's how I allow my feelings to flow…

I don't have the time to indulge in hearsay,
Or in another's opinion anymore.
Too busy building a legacy,
Creating my own doors.

To sum it up,
You cannot hold me, victim
To the things I've already forgiven myself for.

Sing B/C You're Happy, Sing B/C You're Free

To have a song and not sing
Is like wanting to fly when you don't have any wings.

Like wanting to dance about
But feeling like your feet is glued to the ground.
Break free,
Dance,
Make your sound.

For it is your voice,
Use it proudly.
It is your feet that control your ground.

Know who you are,
And where you want to go.

It's your life,
It's your soul.

Atlas

Being overly criticized
Made me defensive,
And easily angered.

Childhood inconsistency
Turned into trauma of paranoia,
Created an inner fear
Of always feeling as if I was in danger…

Experiencing sorrow so cold,
Puddles of it turned into glaciers.

Don't get close to me,
Avoiding the intimacy,
The warmth.
It feels good,
But it doesn't last.

And then …
In the far distance, there it is…
Atlas…
A new beginning.

Act Right

Show me your best behavior…
In my mind,
That's what God's repeating to me.
I'm trying,
So, tell your other creation to stop testing me.

I read the book of Job.

That line was for the old souls…
And for those that don't know,
It's a book that describes how one should handle life when it gets cold.

May you be blessed,
And the goodness you give,
You get back ten-fold.

Stay away from negative souls,
They'll try dimming your light
Because they don't glow.

In my own bubble,
Where evil doesn't exist,
Bad things do not happen to children.
No such thing as a mortgage, car payment or rent…

Everyone allowed in my bubble is filled with joy:

Joy that was found from within.

There You Are

Becoming a parent at the tender age of sixteen was one of the scariest decision I've made. Of course, I would love to say that when this decision was made, I had a solid foundation and was prepared to be the best mother I could be, but that is not the case. Nia's dad and I were thrilled when we found out we had a baby coming, but two children ages sixteen and seventeen were far from ready to be parents. It was the love of our daughter that kept us going, even after we split and did that thing, we all know as co-parenting.

A bit off-topic, but if you're reading this and you're a single parent, co-parent the best way you know (if that option is available). It's not about you, take yourself and your emotions out of it. Children don't care who did what to whom, they want access to both parents. It helps with their development. I understand that all circumstances are different, your child's safety must never be in question, of course.

Now that my daughter is seventeen (past the age I had her) it's as if a new era has begun, and I'm proud to say that at seventeen, one of the greatest things my daughter created and still creates is great artwork. Not to mention she's a phenomenal writer. I'm proud of her and the young lady she's becoming.

Being a parent for most of my life has left me little time to get to know myself. I know I love to write; I've kept a journal and always had a wild imagination (hence the title of my first novel). I also love the art of business. Yes, there's an art to business… there's an art to anything and everything that strikes your passion. My point is everything happens the way it's supposed to. I'm enjoying getting to know myself, *even if it is seventeen years later.*

Better Every Day

We have the power to get better every day,
The only goal is to elevate.
Picked myself up when I was at my lowest state,
But being my protector and my provider has diminished that
thing called feminine energy.

Not taking anything from our creator,
He's always been with me.

I want to get it back,
Feminine energy that is...

But that might not be the plan
Because when masculine and feminine fight,
There's a high chance the masculine's going to win.

But I want to be soft again.
When did it leave?

It might've left when I watched my mother get beat
By this hood rat chick from up the street.
As a young girl couldn't move,
The ground had me by my feet.

It took many years for me to speak about that situation
Because I was so mad at myself.
My mom had my little brother in her hands at the time.

Yes, I was a child,
But I did nothing when she needed me.

Talk about the feeling of defeat.

It might've left when
I was scared to walk home
Because a troubled teen enjoyed harassing me.
He waited at Kingston Ave for me to get off that 3 train.

I couldn't walk home in peace.

It might've left when
I had my baby at sixteen.
So, for her sake and our life,
I had to take the lead…

To mothers, especially young,
This world has no mercy.

Or was it when I had two friends murdered
By the hands of a man?
One was mad because she no longer wanted to dance with him,
And the other, by an old classmate she trusted.

These traumatic experiences are how I know I'm strong
Because I'm still willing to let love in.
But don't mistake my kind heart for weakness,
Within me, a flame is lit.

I'm ready.

To conquer and do what it takes,
So, love it, or leave.
Had to understand the first step to healing
Is forgiving all the negativity I received…
Because it made me,

Me.

Grateful

Times like this,
My mind races.
How do we conquer the battles,
We don't even know we're facing?

Knock 'em down,
One
By
One,
This up North girl is dream chasing.

Must be dreaming,
While I'm awake,
Because I'm loving
My reality.

Young Queen,
Turned into a baby mother,
My daughter didn't like to read.
So, I wrote a book,
And dedicated it to her … "To Nia."

Here,
Read this.

Evolving doesn't come easy.

Grateful for everything,
The way it is.

Snakes and Skin

"Where attention goes, energy flows and results show."

-T. Harv Ever,
Secrets of the Millionaire Mind

Breakthroughs and breakdowns can happen at any moment in life. Normally, I have a breakthrough after a breakdown. I would compare a breakdown to a snake shedding its skin; it can be uncomfortable, and leave us feeling vulnerable, wanting to hide away due to the unknown that change brings. Of course, some individuals embrace change with open arms and live life in the open regardless of the uncertainty. Surrounding myself with those types of people has really opened my eyes and I appreciate every bit of them. They taught me that life is about living and that one should never take themselves too seriously.

My message to you dear reader is to embrace the good
in every situation and let the bad roll off you *like a snake
shedding its skin.*

Vices

I'm a lady,
But sometimes not the lady I aspire to be.
I sometimes drink too much
Because I love the feeling of not giving a f!
About all the B.S. that comes along with adulting.

I'm a lady,
Until I got that Henny in me.
Now my middle finger is up,
Well, because,
Hennessy can make me a little mean.

Can I get a lemon drop
With a tequila that's dark?
Can I get some duce, splash of coke,
Hold the rocks…?

Whiskey,
A gentle kiss when it touches my lips,
A truth teller once it kicks in.
There's always a price to pay when lowering your inhabitations.

This vice is the ish,
But only because I allow it to be.

I pray that I get control over it.
The outcome's never good …

Another Romeo and Juliet,
A forbidden romance,

A tragedy.

Sign of the Times

Cleanse this world,
Let it do away with its negativities…

Allow Summer, Winter, Spring, Fall and rain
To return to its natural state.

Before the term eating organically came to be,
If it's coming from the Earth,
Shouldn't it already be?

Time to get a farm.

Do you all feel how hot it's becoming
outside?
I can hear my mother's voice now,
"Honey, it's the sign of the times."

Message received,
But my mind also lingered on the word,
"Honey".

They come from our bees,
I pray for their well-being while in this heat
Because we sure don't want to miss,

Honey.

Let's try Love!

There's an uproar…
This could mean change is on the way.

Welcome to the United States,
Where one group must stand against oppression
Because the other is fighting not to give their dominant position
away.

I wish everyone would just chill.

<h1 style="text-align:center">Rehabilitate … yeah okay.</h1>

I don't believe in the prison system.
It's inhumane…
Murderers and rapists,
I agree they should be locked away.

But stacked on top of each other,
One hour of sunlight a day.
How exactly is that supposed to rehabilitate?

Demons are what these people are filled with.
Yes, you may call me superstitious
But we need to go back to the days of performing exorcisms,
Proper psychologist who can handle the monsters that these
people live with …
Get into their mind,
With twenty-four-hour proper supervision
In the right type of environment.

Just my opinion.

I have had friends that were murdered.
So, I understand wanting someone buried under a jail.
But them rotting in a cell
Will not help you heal.

Just my opinion.

Build It,
They Will Come.

I wrote a poem titled *Treasure,* inspired by a novel titled *The Alchemist*. The tale follows a young shepherd boy searching for his treasure, his wealth. It was a dream he had that led him on his journey. This book was exceptionally inspiring because it made me think about my very own personal legend. We often think we need to have a certain amount of money or, today, a high social following to accomplish our goals, but that is not the case. Like in *The Alchemist,* I'm finding that the journey is the reward, and the result of getting through our journey is just the icing on the cake.

"Anything worth building takes time, focus and dedication. Your dreams deserve nothing less."

-Eleanor Brown

This Little Light

What day is it?
My mornings are running into my nights.
The world is spinning while I'm creating my own
Far from reality
When I write.

I would love to be present
When I'm on break.

You'll see me outside more
Going to shows and
Frequenting the gym…

But then,
It becomes time to lock in …
I disappear again,
Present, but not.

Job on the line
Because I can't work around their clock;
My characters need developing,
My readers need a brilliant plot,
And my mind's constantly thinking about what's next.
I must zone out the world to be at my best.

No appetite for food,
Characters running too wild in my mind for rest.

Scenes and situations pop up at any time in my head,
Stop everything,
Must grab some paper and pen…

Quiet, to my thoughts I must listen.

I'm the greatest writer of my time,
Billion-dollar goals for Lilac Sky.
Gift given from the most - high,
I pray that He brightens this little light

Of mine.

Transformation Takes Time

"...Created by the great divine,
Handcrafted in time,
Battles you've conquered,
Top of hills you've climbed..."
        -Happiness is Contagious, Father, May I: Collection I
Transformation takes time;
It's never 1...2...3...

Analogy...
It takes 2 to 4 weeks
For a caterpillar
To develop in its cocoon.

And with their lifespan being
8 to 9 months,
Compare that to a human being.

I know the words; I understand the analogy...
So, tell me
Why does it feel so
guilty to rest?

A world
Where I can relax,
Do what I love,
And make money.
And can I get a snap for maintaining inner peace...

Energy going to the things that feed my soul,
And doing what you love is a style that never gets old?

Sending chills up spines,
How my style is so cold…

I know the words,
Thinking bigger,
Going after all that I'm worth.
Life's a journey of discovering why we're put on this Earth.
I read that it starts with putting God first.

I understand, but still,
Why does it feel so guilty to rest?

Treasure

Why aren't I a billionaire yet?
It must be a conspiracy!
No…
I'm just still on my journey.

As in the main character from "The Alchemist" …
I too am on my personal legend.

Enjoying life,
Learning to say yes to opportunities more so than no,
Can't help it though.
I'm just a solo player who likes to get in her zone,
Outer and inner wrestling,
Warm on the inside,
But the appearance is stone cold.
Another spirit takes over when I speak my poems;
She's a beast from Brooklyn
Coming with an intense tone,
Building her legacy with every stone that was thrown.
Focused,
Because time is of the essence when accomplishing goals.

It's my life
And I want to live free…
And for that
I don't need to be a billionaire just yet.

But wouldn't it sure make it easy.

Self–Regulator

Discipline…

You are bittersweet,

The trick and the treat,

Needed so in this world,

One can compete.

How else will we become the best versions of ourselves the world has yet to see?

*"Creativity
takes Courage."*

-Henri Matisse

Nia Figueroa

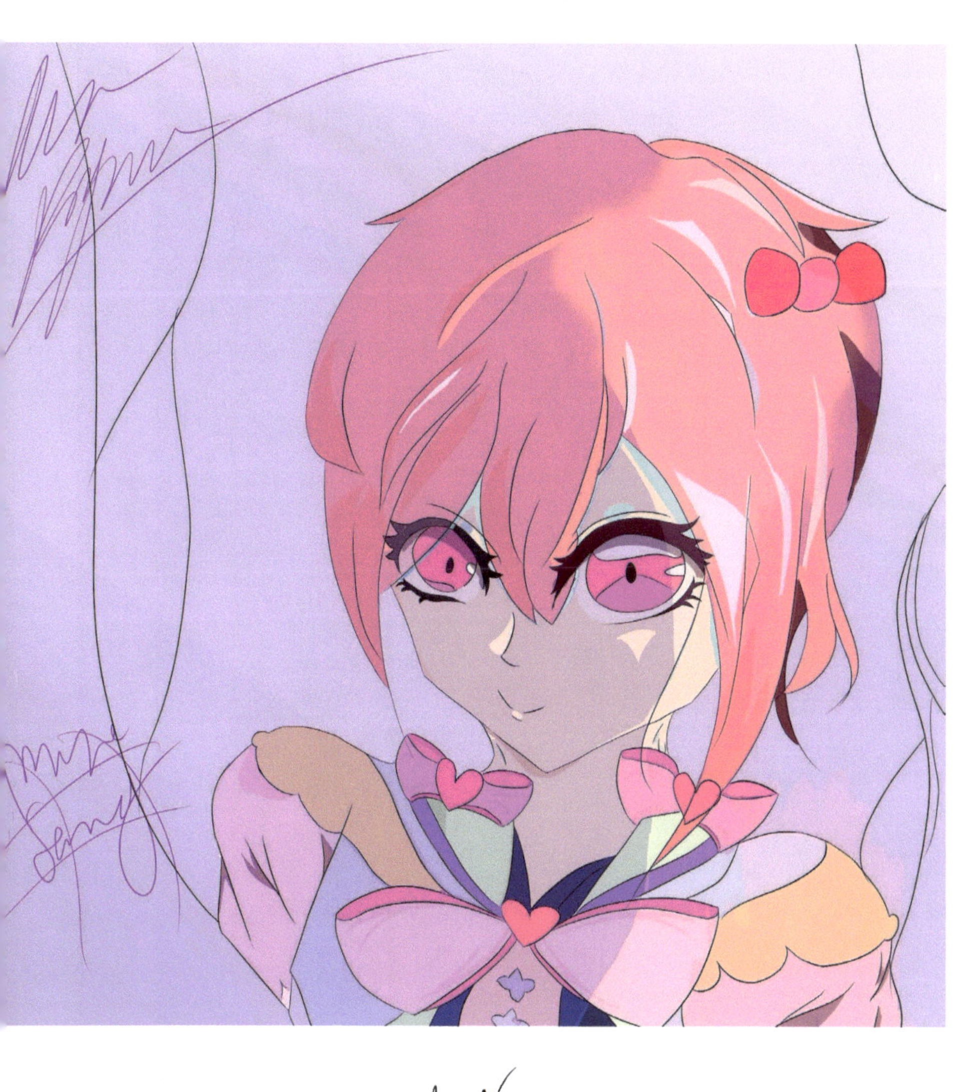

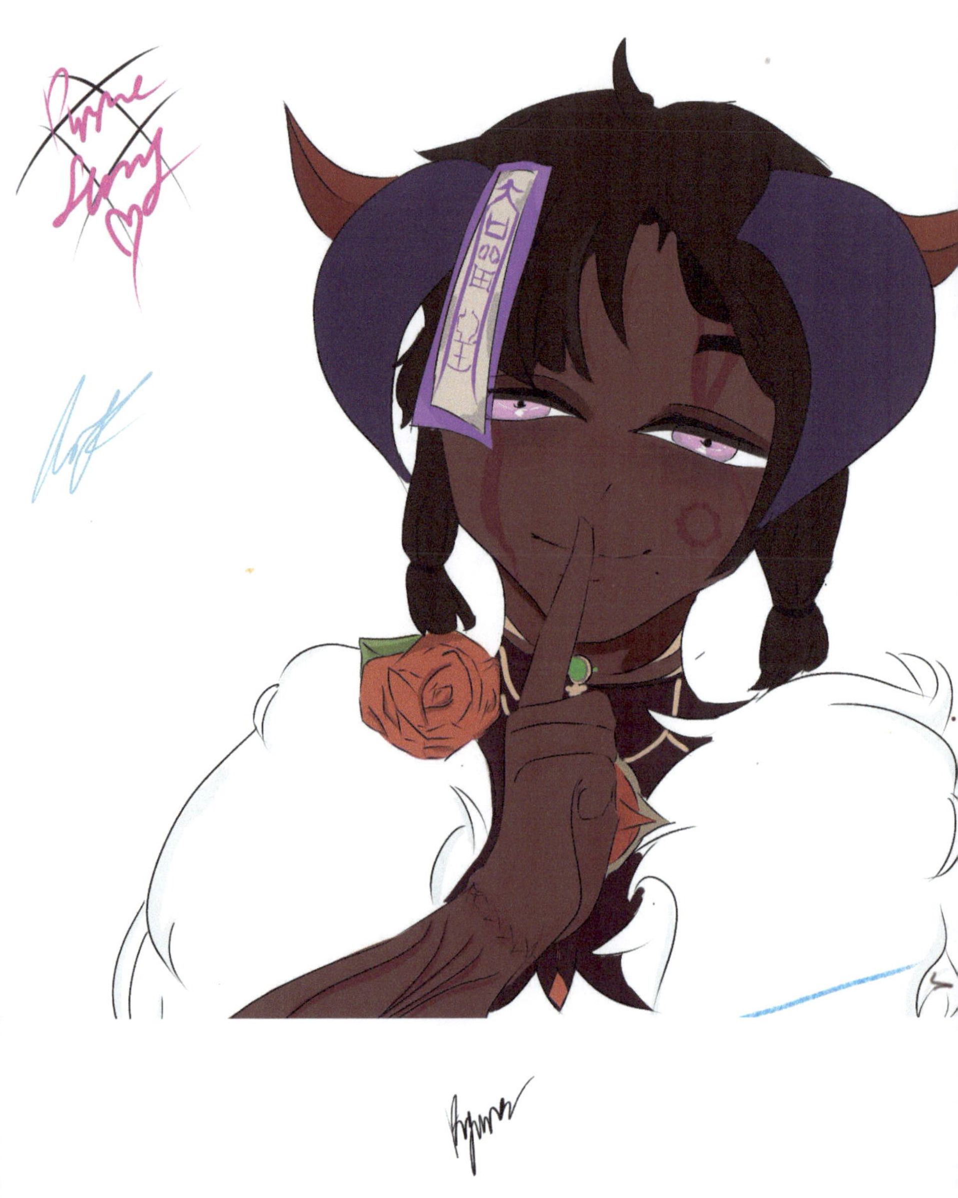

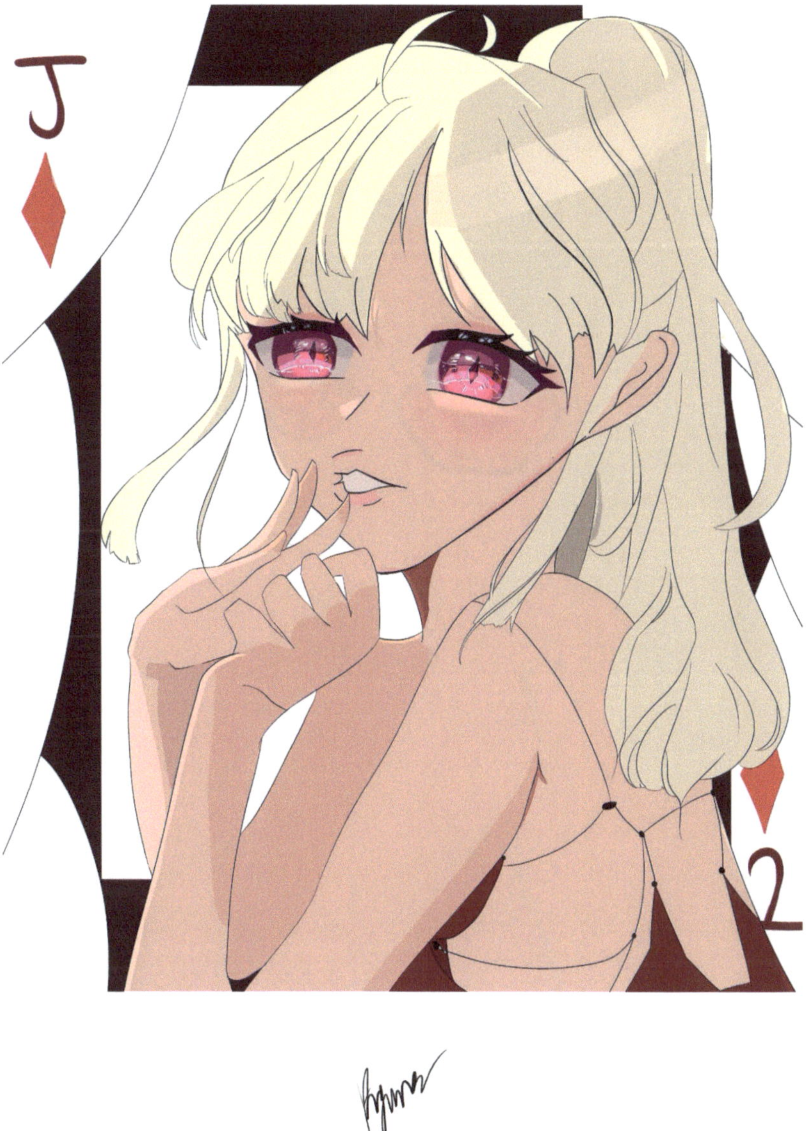

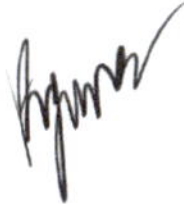

A Poem About New York
Nia Figueroa

The sounds of New York are always clamorous.
The sparkling city lights were glamorous.
The city was bustling,
But the trees were not in
sight,
For all of them were gone
In the anchor of the smite.
The streets were dangerous,
But the corner stores were trusting,
For neither did they sleep
Adding to the never-ending diluted sense of peace.
Throughout all the violence, there is still a promise within the breeze.
The energy and hopefulness in the eyes of people
Was always just enough for me.

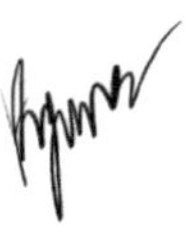

Location: Norway – Past

Our story begins with the telling of Kampen's preschool life. At this time of his life, he was absent from both his parents ... being an orphan his entire life, he developed a sense that he didn't belong because of the attention he'd see his peers get. Bearing the weight of going to the nearby public school, along with the other orphans was crushing for all of them; but the city at the time was too poor to install an orphan school for the group.

At the age of 16, Kampen's loneliness had been accompanied by a companion whose name was Víðarr. These two, described by teachers and others, were both hermits who only hung out with each other. On a gloomy, cloudy day, the two had been at recess with the other children, but not in the same area as them. They stood on the roof of the school building. Their feet were dangling.

As they spoke, a cackle and rumble halted their voices made by an explosion that came from the near distance. Both Kampen and Víðarr were frozen in their spots before the distant screams of others in the area could be heard; the children ran back into school for safety. Kampen quickly snatched the arm of his best friend and busted through the door, running down their school stairs where they ran into their teachers who scurried to collect their students; escorting them to the basement, their voices were silenced by the constant horrified screams.

It wasn't too long before another bomb set off. This time, a closer explosion was heard followed by an immense amount of gunfire. Kampen's knees shook as he stood with Víðarr, not knowing what to do. The voices of others were drowned out at this point. Kampen turned to his friend, who looked equally terrified, but to a point where it was hard to walk, noticing his trembling knees, and glued feet. His very first instinct was to hug him as tight as he could.

That day, millions were escorted out of their homes and put in safety camps. However, only a handful of orphans went to those safety camps. In the process of this, soldiers attempted to split the two up. Víðarr was to be escorted to a safety camp while Kampen was to be taken elsewhere– to which he viciously opposed, and both refused to let go of each other's hands. The soldiers came to an agreement with Víðarr and Kampen, escorting them elsewhere together, along with other orphans that hadn't been picked for the safety camp.

They were transported by bus, where the two friends silently sat close together, afraid to be removed from one another for a single second. As they arrived at their destination, it was painfully obvious that the elsewhere the soldiers discussed was a military camp. For a long, grueling 6 months of training, all those who were transported were trained for war. Both Kampen and Víðarr were not the same young men who were dangling their feet from the school's roof.

Three years later, the war was still raging, and the two boys were now men and were still best friends. On June 15th, they'd been sent on another mission in the Northwest. On the ride there, not a peep was made, understanding the severity with this being their third deployment, Kampen held Víðarr's hand firmly until their carriage was suddenly ambushed. It flipped, and the soldiers inside were thrown outside of their carriage due to a bomb their enemy attacked them with.

With blurred vision, Kampen opened his eyes to see his comrades injured, he spotted Víðarr through the many bodies that surrounded him. He managed to crawl his way to his friend, who was hanging from the now-damaged carriage they were just riding in. Kampen, who was injured himself managed to firmly grip his friend's hand. Víðarr turned his aching body to face him; his eyes were low. Kampen yelled at him to get up as the shooting started, but Víðarr softly shook his head, and placed a hand on Kampen's cheek. Although he had a violent sense of urgency, he looked at his best friend with a sense of confusion and relaxation. Kampen shook his head, realizing what was to come, as Víðarr slowly allowed the words "leave me, get out of here," slowly and lowly leave his lips.

Those words shattered Kampen, and immediately, he shook his head with tears in his eyes. He pulled his friend off the carriage and was able to get one arm around his shoulder, "Hold me," said Kampen getting the two out of harm's way, when he saw wooden boats near a body of water that were stopped at shore.

Without another thought he made a run for it, attempting to move past the eyes of anyone else and luckily, he did. The gunfire was still harrowing, for no matter how many tours were taken, Kampen had not grown numb to it. He placed his friend on one of the small boats, and took a closer look at him, observing his wounds.

"Okay…it doesn't look bad, I can get this fixed right when we..." As Kampen spoke, he looked up at his friend to where he was looking for his eyes, but his eyes weren't the same. He wasn't here anymore. Kampen silently sat on the boat with his friend, and rode to wherever it took them.

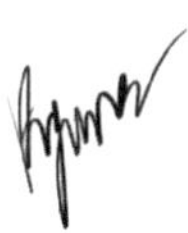

About the Author

My name is Nia Figueroa and I've been a writer since the age of 8 years old, and I am currently 18. I started writing when I discovered something called roleplaying, and I haven't stopped ever since. Music is one of my bigger passions! I adore music. Every genre - it does not matter to me. I love playing horror games, watching horror movies, anything horrific. My big passion in life is to either pursue my writing as a career or pursue law as a career. I love both of these routes.

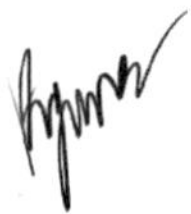

Tori L. Edwards

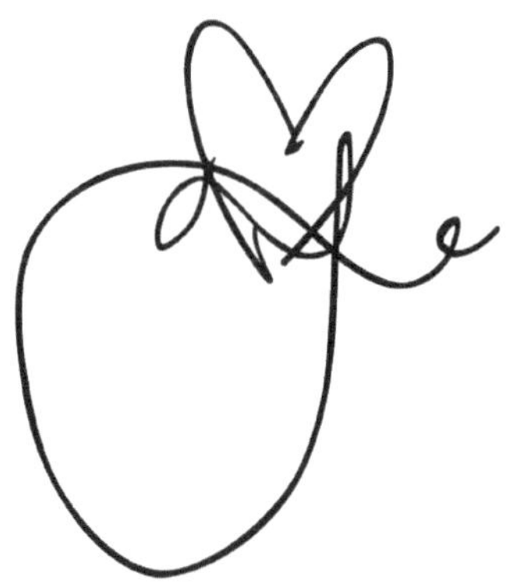

Bounded
Tori L. Edwards

Bounded by love,
Bounded by ink.
My sister,
My confidant,
All the things
in-between
these words I share,
Are my living testimony.
Embracing my lows
Embracing my highs
has catapulted me.
My sister,
My
confidant,
All the things
in-between,
I cherish our union.
It's the sisterhood
That inspires me.

About the Author

Tori L. Edwards began her journey in Atlanta, GA. Rooted in faith, her walk is the evidence of grace. Her story is a testament to surmounting the odds. The legacy she builds today is affording her the opportunity to achieve great heights. At 28 years old, Tori L. Edwards is a *Self-Published Author, Speaker, and Project Manager for The MOTHA Project.* Tori debuted her acting career in Lucy's House Entertainment: Momma Don't Count Me Out Stage Play in the spring of 2024. She looks forward to expressing herself creatively in ways that will challenge her to dig deeper. Over the years Tori L. Edwards has led charitable movements for group homes. She has blessed platforms by sharing her wisdom. **Present-day,** Tori L. Edwards is continuing to revolutionize communities through writing and teaching about emotional intelligence, unity, and love.

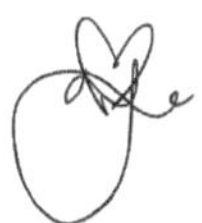

Talon Baker

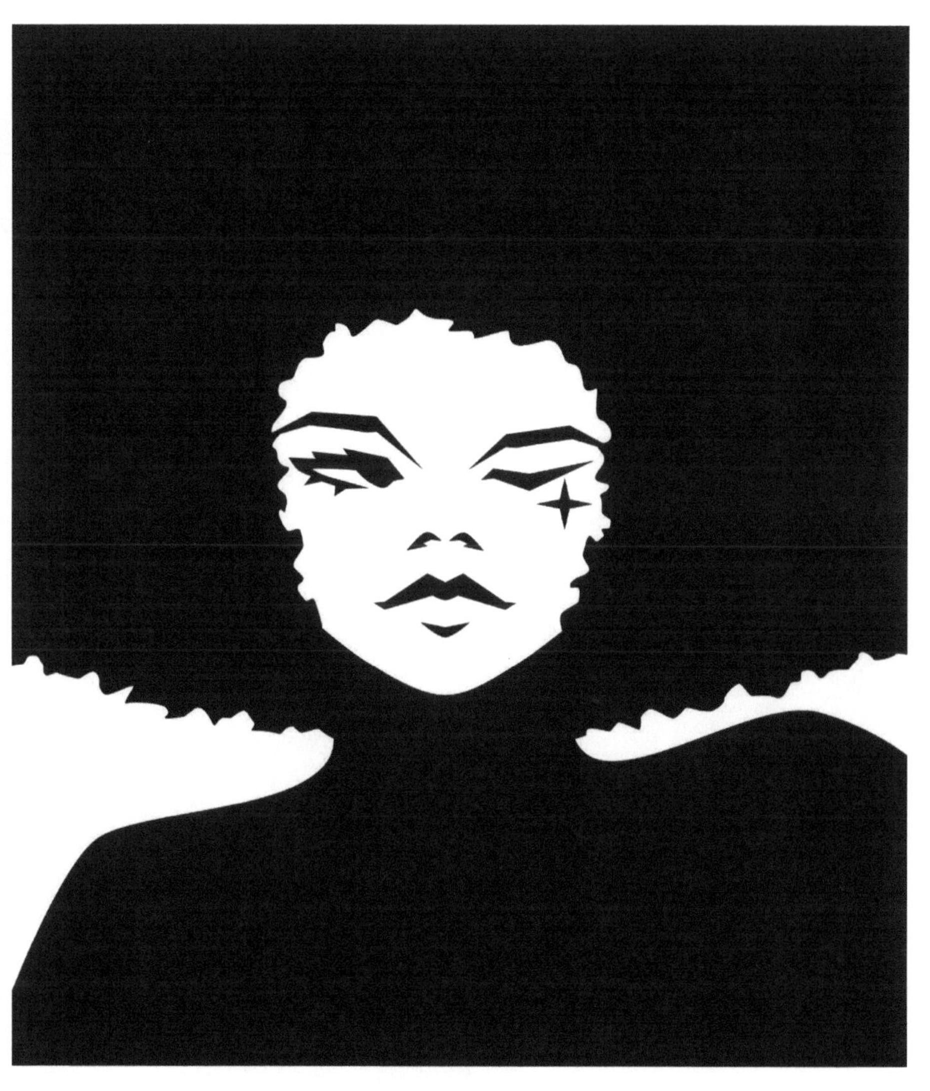

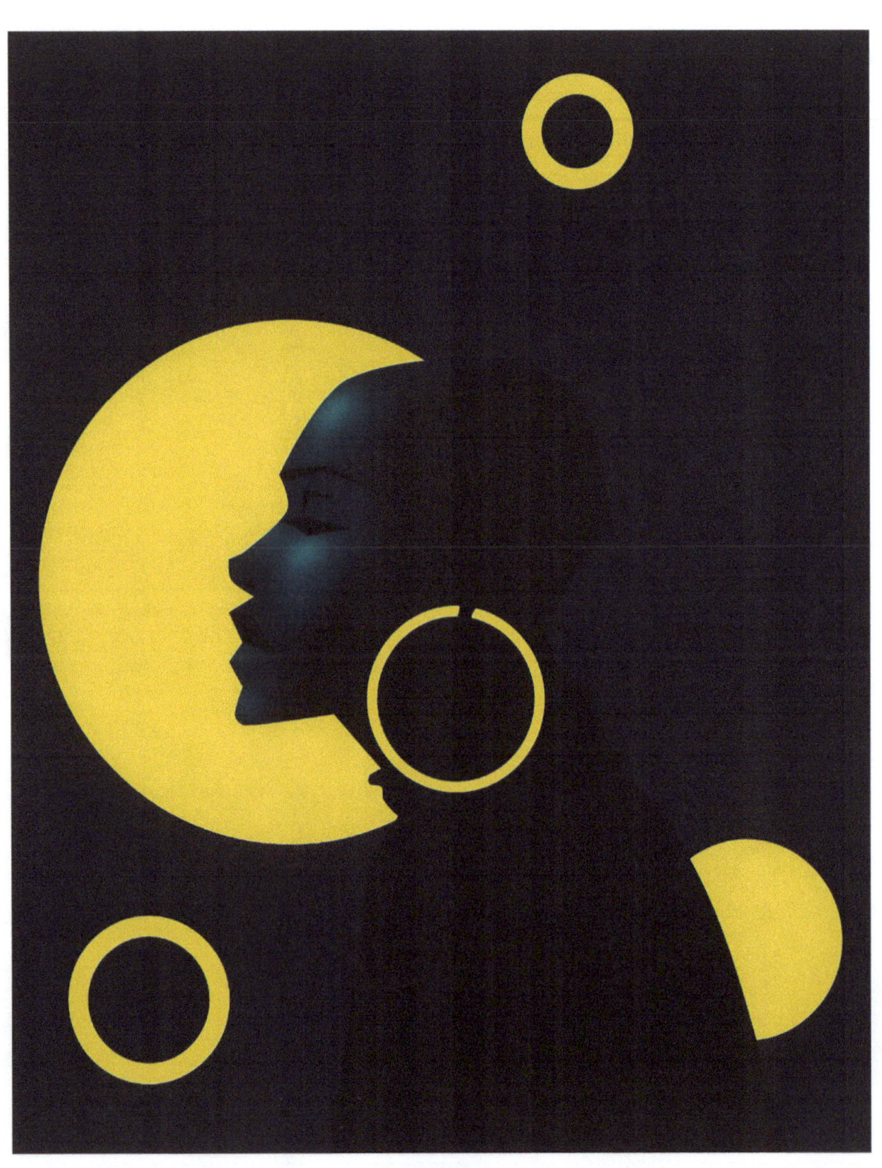

About the Author

My name is Talon Baker, and I am a **self-taught artist**, with a strong drive for creativity. Some of the contributions I've made were creating flyers for the nonprofit organization, *Kids Drone Zone* in 2020, and I designed the mascot for my former high school, Global Impact Academy. I have been drawn to art for as long as I can remember, and I know that my passion will only grow stronger from here.

Christain Hunt

You're Worth It
By: Christain Hunt

Life is a portrait
With its many images.
People change every day.
Explaining it would only turn into a run-on sentence.

Must live in the moment to paint the image.

So much destruction within oneself
Must pay attention to how you're living.

All this killing needs to stop!
Life is a joy
That deserves to be lived.
Must be mentally strong to make it to the top.

Focus on your health
And your days will be long.
Take control of your emotions
And engage with things that keep you mentally strong.

About the Author

Hi, my name is Christain Hunt. I'm currently on active duty in the Navy and, I'm also a rapper/artist who goes by *"Ranaj"*. I joined the Navy to build a foundation for a better future and to make the world a better place. Music is my overall passion. I love to write music that moves people and connects to others. My main goal is to help others grow and feel secure within themselves.

*In the words of Toni Braxton,
Let it Flow.*

We all have an escape when we need peace. I have many and one of them is water; it doesn't matter if it's a bath, shower, my toes in the ocean, or tubing down a river - all I know is water has a way of calming me. I recall a time when my family and I were tubing down the Chattahoochee River; we tied our tubes together so we wouldn't separate and would be able to collectively kick away from the rocks to avoid running into them. We were successful until one rock snuck underneath me and boom, out of the tube I went, trying to catch my balance on the very rock that took me out. The moss on the rock made it difficult, but I managed. As I stood there, in the middle of the Chattahoochee River, standing on this sneaky boulder, I watched my family drift away from me. Their attempts to get to rescue me were short-lived due to the pulling current.

In a situation where I was knocked off course, and nearly stranded, I thought I would've been frightened, but I wasn't. An indescribable calm quickly took over. I looked around and noticed all the tubes, rafts, and kayaks all looking at me, fear written on their faces. Moments later, there was a group of young adults tubing who saw me stranded, and their tubes began drifting in my direction (with some extra help from the passengers). I was amazed by how much ease it came, because if you know anything about currents, you know they're not easy to go against. Not only that, but the current also didn't fight us too hard with getting me back to my tube and family.

We thanked the group that saved me, grateful that they were there, but also amazed at how the tube came over to me as if the current knew I needed a hand and the willingness of the passengers to make sure I returned to my family safe.

Our setbacks represent getting knocked out of our tubes. Here we are, just going through life, and then boom, next thing we're standing on a rock, (which represents our hard place in life), watching others pass us by; but there's no need to panic. Sooner or later, the current will shift in our favor, and the passengers represent the great people we meet along the way.

Music

I love music…
Yes, some of the lyrics express the negative,
But artists are free to create art from their perspectives. And
there're some lyrics with a positive message.

Sade for the chill.

Jazz when I'm in my mind…
Don't always need the lyrics.
For me,
It's the sound of the instruments combined.

Battle rap…
Artists who let their pen transform everyday words
That will leave you in awe.
Their delivery is authentic, creative, and raw.

African music…
Can't help but move my waist to the rhythmic
beat,
Quickest way to get me out of my seat.

Can never forget R&B of course,
My faves…
If named,
This piece would be too long.

Music, the universal language of the world.

In My Heart

Though getting to know you brings upon many questions.
It doesn't change how I feel about your existence
Because I'm learning that these questions come to my attention.

They're many theories of who you are,
And what your name could be.
But I know you as Father God,
The one who created the universe and my ancestors,

Who guide and protect me.

It Is What it Is.

I 'm at a point in my life
Where the motto is…
It is what it is.

No flight or fight,
Just controlling what I can control,
Taking the necessary steps to accomplish my goals,
Surrounded by pure,
Good, intended souls…
And if they're not,
It is what it is.

God on my side,
Turning these bullies into so-called victims.
Born stubborn,
So, I had to learn to listen.

Everything's a lesson,
Grateful for every decision,
Because always,

It is what it is.

Brooklyn to Atlanta

hat not a better teacher than life?

W I am from New York … Brooklyn to be exact and I now live in Atlanta. Like most of us from the city of New York, driving can be a hassle, and with the amount of public transportation, obtaining a car is optional, but that was not the case when I moved to Georgia. Let me say that Atlanta does have public transportation, but if you'll be traveling to the outskirts of Atlanta, you need a car. So, there I was, fresh out of New York into another state with no car and no money to get one. So, I decided to work for a car dealership to familiarize myself with cars, and what it takes to maintain a car as far as maintenance, cost, and insurance are concerned… you get where I'm going? Plus, I knew that if I worked for the dealership, I would get a deal on my vehicle. It was a win-win.

Now, I left out a very important detail in this story and that's the fact that I didn't even know how to drive my dear reader. Yes!

I was twenty-nine years old, just received my driver's license and now, it was time for a car, but didn't have much experience behind the wheel! This is a blog and not my memoir, so I will not go into detail as to what it was like obtaining my driver's license… that will be a story for next time. I found the car of my dreams and I was able to purchase it, one of the happiest days of my life until it became time to hit the highway.

If you don't know what it's like driving on Highway 285, just watch NASCAR. I was terrified, I would grip the wheel so hard, that I began to get calluses on my hands. However, I was determined to get better, I had no choice. I would constantly pray to God to make me better and to protect me while I'm on the road (still do). I called my dad one day after having a breakdown (due to an incident that I will also save for another time), and asked him, "How do I become a better driver?" My dad said to me "The key is repetition. The more you do something, the better you'll be at it." I heard this same thing at *Atlanta Invest Vest of 2023*. I continued driving despite fear and now, you can't pull me away. I love driving and have become quite good at it.

When I heard the speaker give the advice my dad gave me, I believed it, not only because I heard it twice, but also because life has proven that statement to be true. Learning how to drive is just one example of that. Whatever you want to achieve, just keep at it … in the words of my dad, *repetition is key.*

You're Doing Good versus Not Good Enough

Got no time to be playing with you.
Are you meeting my standards?
Been through too much,
Not to raise the bar…

Moved from another state,
Much love to Brother B.
No time to rest
Because nothing worth having comes easy.

Got two sides to me battling,
Nu Jerzey Twork…
For my future, I'm strapped in,
Inner being I'm channeling.

I not only came to play,
I came to win.

ATL Wassup

Living out here has been a whole vibe.
Black Hollywood at its finest…
Where creators are not hard to find.
This city's culture is rich,
Home of lemon pepper wings,
And where I discovered grits.

Yes,
The traffic is crazy,
But in any major city that's bound to exist.
Home of *MLK* and *Georgia Me*,
And waffle house …
Let me get a bacon egg on a Texas melt, with cheese.

Leaders,
Let's come correct with it,
Normalize following our passions and dreams.
Stop the killing and be more willing to walk away from
situations that try to steal our peace.

Doing what you love doesn't always come easy,
But nothing worth having does…
Let's normalize not looking for outside approval,
And give that attention to the one above.

This city has become a melting pot,
And we are all here for a reason…

Atlanta … I love the city I live in.

Lady Boss

Artists are different,
And people fear what they don't understand,
An innately nonstop burning to be great,
We can't help it,
It's God's plan.

Society does not cater to the brilliant mind
Until that mind does something impactful.
Until then,
You're just another soul trying to make your dreams come alive.

All I know is that I wanted to write,
So, I created Lilac Sky…

I believe in me,
Going to be the biggest lady boss you ever did see,
The beast in me needs to feast.

She's hungry.

Sweet Tea

My name is Narell…
Spelled with one "r"
Beyonce said it best.
Too classy for this world,
I'm an alien superstar.

Born and raised in New York,
And moving to the South grew me
up.
The slow pace and isolation
Allowed for some traumas to heal up.

I love the South
But upon arrival,
I learned another meaning to the words:
Sweet Tea.

You may think they're being nice,
But can't help but notice the undertone of nasty.
Yeah baby,
You've had a taste of the southern *sweet tea.*

It's cool, that's your attitude;
Has nothing to do with me.

What Skeleton

A king comes to his Queen, disgruntled about rumors concerning his wife having sexual dealings with a man from the village. Now, the king is a secure man, but hearing stories about his wife with another man, is something the king would rather not hear. The Queen tries to deny, but the king is adamant that it happened.

"Why do you deny me of truth?" The woman pleads…
Because there's only one way to describe it,
And he did…

"Well,
What did he say?"

"He described it as …

Amazing.
Had him in another galaxy,
Star gazing. "

"I'm not sure if even know this man,
And your accusations are almost making me feel shame and regret.
And I quite don't like that.
It's you who I'm with now.
It's you whose back I have.

Before barging in,
Did you consider that you'll become friends?"

The King didn't quite like that,
But liked everything else she said.
He simply kissed her on the forehead,
Then walked off,
Just shaking his head.

Sour Patch Kid

Hun,
If I knew what to give,
I would give it to you.
I just have ways of being
mean,
And nice
At the same time.

I'm just a big ol' sour patch kid.
But my love is so yummy,
It's going to make you wanna chew.

Like Brandy,
Writing love songs while I'm
Sitting up in my room.

Question,
Do we ever fully heal?
Or…
Do we just learn better ways to deal?

I don't know.
So…
Bring all that ish with you…
Bet we make it through.

Better yet,

We'll thrive.
Just as long as you can remember,
That I have ways of being mean,
And nice
At the same time.

No More Second Guessing

Once you make a decision,
Stand on it.

But that can become tricky with love,
Especially when the heart just wants
What the heart wants.

Irrational decision making…
All emotion, some brain
Must be all brain these days.

But unless it disrespects your integrity, morals, or values,
Stand on the decision you've made
Trust yourself
And walk with
Faith.

Empath

Empaths …
Great at touching the insecure parts of people they don't see,
Have individuals walking on top of the Earth,
Appreciating their inner being.

How do they do such a thing?
By listening,
Putting themselves in another's position,
Wanting to heal the wounds of others,
Deep seeded root to want to take away another's trauma.

If they only knew that's not possible…
Be careful that no one takes advantage of you.
If a person wants to heal,
They will…

Be sure that your cup is also being fulfilled.

Sodom and Gomorrah

There's a plague happening,
Though most can't see.

Sex is everywhere;
Media tries to dumb it down
As if it's nothing,
Normalizing the transferring of energy,
Normalize us sleeping around.

Performing that sacred act allows entrance not only into your body,
But also, your mind and spirit.
But somewhere along the line,
We stopped looking at it like that.

It's imperative that we open our eyes and see
There's a plague happening
Just like in the ancient cities.
They're calling it sexual liberation,
And, if in it do I believe?

Heck no,
The act of lovemaking is too precious to be taken so lightly.
Never to be toyed with or taken for granted…
For it is the highest form of passion,
And it should be respected.

I'm not trying to preach,
Just passing along a message.

Catch a Flight

So much of this world
That I have not yet seen;
I am surely looking forward to doing more traveling…

See the world with the closest of close
By my side,
Sharing new experiences,
Broadening our minds,
I look forward to such a time.

A Writer's Wish

Positive feedback
Expressing that my book is on fire.
I hope it inspires people
To reach heights never thought possible.

I write because I love it
And because I have stories I want to share
That explains darkness to be temporary;
Messages that explain of the light ahead,
Where chaos exists
Only to mess with our heads.

Where our decisions are our choice,
And they'll certainly lead us down a path,
Where being our greatest self is the only thing
Our Ruler asks.

Just My Imagination and *Father, May I* is a small percentage of
the things that go on in my mind.

Throughout my journey,
I wish to create a fanbase,
An audience who will ride,
Their loyalty will stand the test of time.

Epilogue

"*Bounded by Ink*" is a melting pot of creative evolution, the blending of your passion for writing, with an appreciation for publishing. The incorporation of artwork from other artists adds an intriguing dimension marking a milestone in my publishing career, with this novel being the third one published.

It was a vibrant journal of a young Anastasia from the "Hunch Back of Notre Dame" dancing on the front cover, a gift from my grandmother, which sprouted the roots of my writing journey. I didn't recognize it back then, but finishing one journal and moving onto the next, symbolized moving on from one chapter of my life to the next … the cyclical nature of growth and evolution.

Becoming a mother in my middle teens shifted my priorities, landing me in the legal and social service field; but fueled with determination to pursue my passion for writing despite the challenges, I didn't let my dream stray too far.

Returning to writing professionally, culminating in the publication of *"Bounded by Ink: Collection II"*, is a testament to perseverance and dedication to my craft. My hope is that *"Bounded by Ink: Collection II"* reminds us that our passion has a way of finding us, even amidst life's trials and tribulations.

Cheers to you reader, I wish you continued success and the fulfillment of your creative dreams.

About the Author

*Narell Hunt's journey from New York City to Atlanta is the journey
that transformed her into a writer and entrepreneur.
Her debut novel, "Just My Imagination," released in 2020
during the pandemic, explores the theme of choices and their
impact on our lives, emphasizing the possibility of
redemption and returning to one's true self.*

*Following her successful entry into the literary world through
another medium with the release of "Father, May I: Collection II"
in 2022. This poetry novel delves into personal messages and
reflections, offering readers a deeper connection
through emotional expression.*

*Beyond her own creative pursuits, Narell's entrepreneurial spirit
led her to establish Lilac Sky Publishing, LLC, a platform dedicated
to collaborating with artists who have a creative gift to share.
Her venture expanded into merchandise with the launch
of the "Shh, I'm Writing" line of journals in 2023,
catering to fellow writers and creatives.*

*She hopes that her life story and work will resonate with those
who hear it, wanting it to be a testament to the power
of embracing one's creativity and passion and sharing
it with beautiful minds like you.*

End